994
A11
C.1

Allison, Robert J.

Australia

DATE DUE	BORROWER'S NAME	ROOM NUMBER
	Ashley	214
	Clara M	382
2/27/03	Jose Escoto	204
5/12/04	Jazmin M	204

994
A11
C.1

Allison, Robert J.

Australia

AUSTRALIA

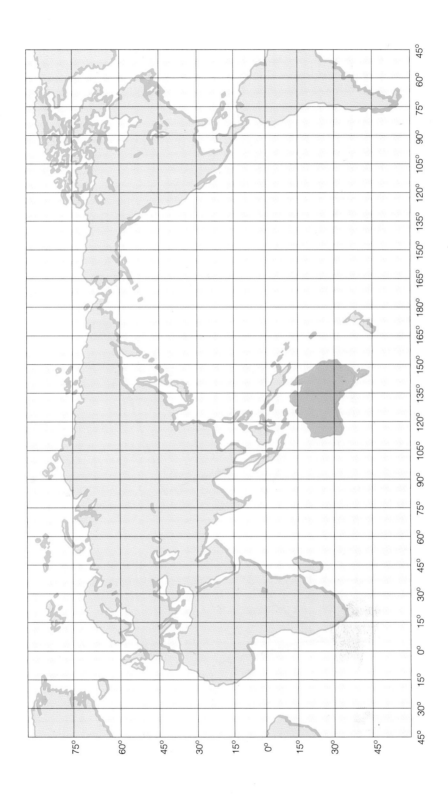

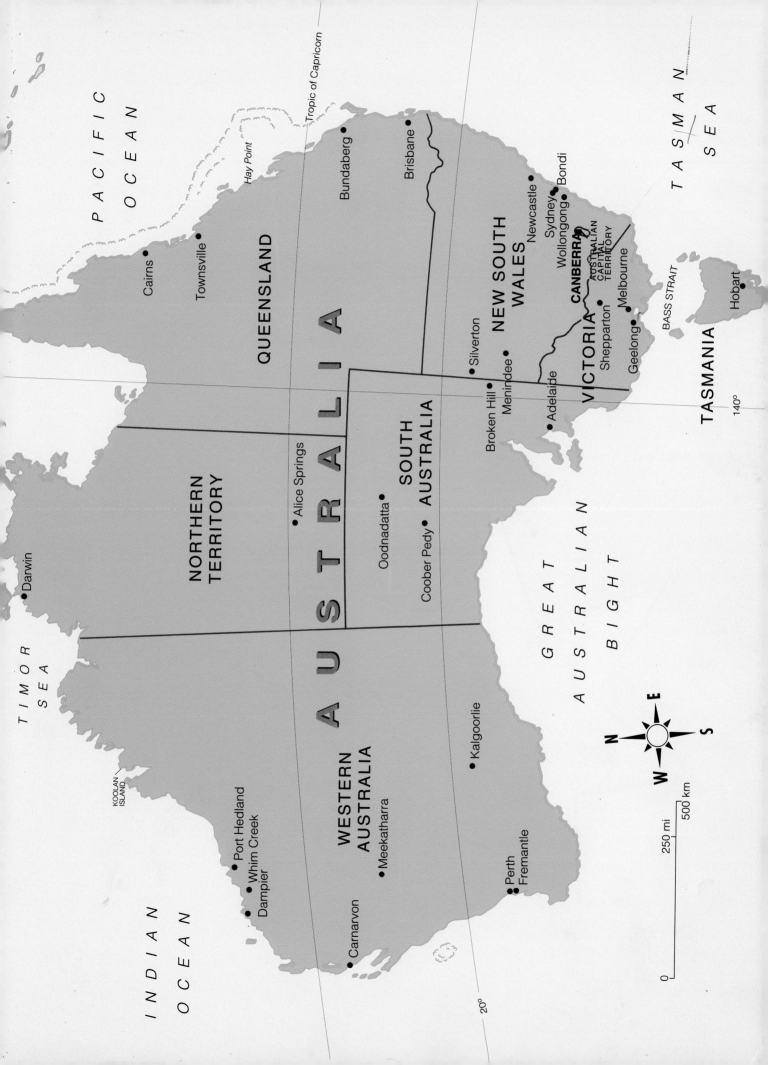

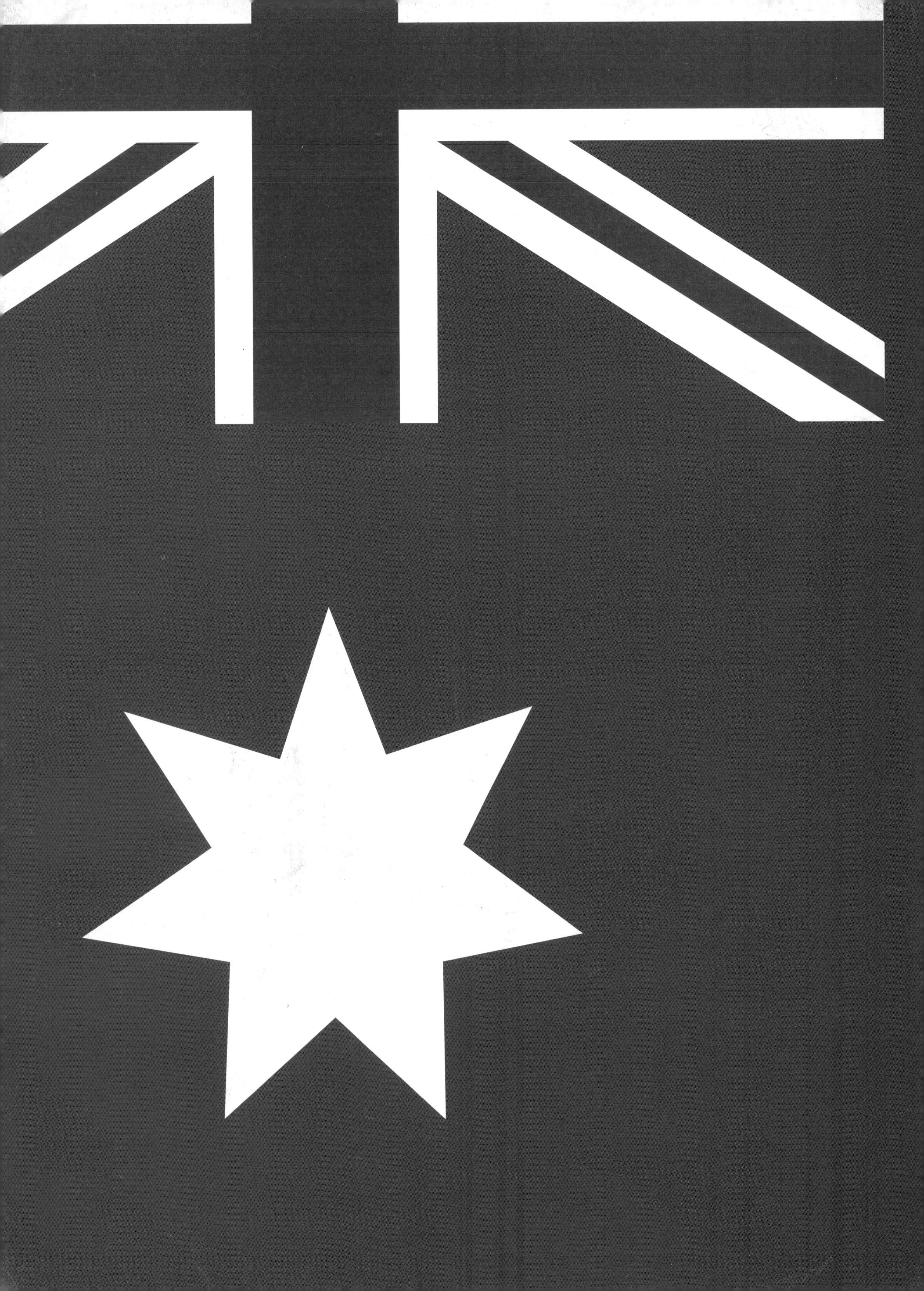

AUSTRALIA

Robert J. Allison

RAINTREE STECK-VAUGHN
PUBLISHERS

Austin, Texas

Text © Robert J. Allison 1995
All rights reserved. No part of this book may be reproduced or
utilized in any form or by any means, electronic or mechanical,
including photocopying, recording, or by any information
storage and retrieval system, without permission in writing
from the Publisher. Inquiries should be addressed to:
Copyright Permissions,
Steck-Vaughn Company,
P.O. Box 26015,
Austin, TX 78755
Published by Raintree Steck-Vaughn Publishers, an imprint of
Steck-Vaughn Company

Design	Roger Kohn
Editors	Diana Russell, Shirley Shalit
DTP editor	Helen Swansbourne
Picture research	Valerie Mulcahy
Illustration	János Márffy
	Malcolm Porter
Consultant	Dr. Philip Hirsch
Commissioning editor	Debbie Fox

We are grateful to the following for permission
to reproduce photographs:
Front Cover: Joanne Fox *above,* Zefa *below;*
Allsport (UK) Ltd, page 24 *above right* (Bob Martin); Colorific!,
pages 35 and 40 *above* (Bill Bachman); Robert Harding Picture
Library, pages 38/39; The Image Bank, page 24 *above left*
(Don & Liysa King); Mitsubishi Motors Australia Ltd, page 32;
Spectrum Colour Library, pages 11 *above,* 17 *right* and 18/19
below (Diana Calder), 18/19 *above* (G Adsett), 33, 39 and 41
(D. & J. Heaton), 40 *below;* Tony Stone Images, pages 11
below (Chesley), 20 (Fritz Prenzel), 36 *below* (B. Chittock);
Sygma, pages 17 *left* (J. Guichard), 29 *below* (Rick Smolan);
TRIP/Eye Ubiquitous, pages 27 and 42 *above* (Matthew
McKee), 29 *above* (J. Winkley), 43 (Sportshoot); TRIP, page
37 (T. Knight); TRIP/Robin Smith, pages 8 *above,* 12, 14, 15,
16, 21, 22 *below,* 23, 24 *below,* 26, 28 *left* and *right,* 30, 31,
34, 36 *above,* 42 *below;* Zefa, pages 8/9, 10, 22 *above*
(Boiselle), 25 (Damm).

The statistics given in this book are the most up to date
available at the time of going to press.

Printed in Hong Kong by Wing King Tong

2 3 4 5 6 7 8 9 0 HK 99 98 97

Library of Congress Cataloging-in-Publication Data
Allison, R.J. (Robert J.)
Australia / Robert J. Allison.
p. cm. – (Country fact files)
Includes bibliographical references (p.44) and index.
Summary: Describes the landscape, climate, natural
resources, culture, and industry of Australia.
ISBN 0-8114-5642-0
1. Australia – Juvenile literature. (1. Australia)
I. Title. II. Series.
DU96.A48 1996
994–dc20
95-31308
CIP AC

INTRODUCTION page **8**

THE LANDSCAPE page **10**

CLIMATE AND WEATHER page **12**

NATURAL RESOURCES page **16**

POPULATION page **18**

DAILY LIFE page **22**

RULES AND LAWS page **26**

FOOD AND FARMING page **28**

TRADE AND INDUSTRY page **32**

TRANSPORTATION page **36**

THE ENVIRONMENT page **38**

THE FUTURE page **42**

FURTHER INFORMATION page **44**
GLOSSARY page **44**
INDEX page **45**

**C
O
N
T
E
N
T
S**

Words that are explained in the glossary are printed in
SMALL CAPITALS the first time they are mentioned in the text.

■ INTRODUCTION

Australia lies between latitudes 10°S and 44°S and longitudes 112°E and 154°E. It is a vast country, stretching some 2,286 miles (3,680 km) from north to south and 2,485 (4,000 km) from east to west.

The original inhabitants of Australia were the Aborigines, a dark-skinned people whose lifestyle is closely linked with the land and natural environment. They were the sole inhabitants of the island continent until 1788, when a boat from England arrived at what is now Sydney Harbor. The boat was full of convicts and many of the first white settlers were prisoners who had been banished from Britain and sent to the "other side of the world" for the rest of their lives. Gradually, people started to emigrate to Australia of their own free choice, and today the country is inhabited

▲An Aborigine in a cave at Uluru (Ayers Rock), a traditional sacred site of Australia's original inhabitants.

▼Sydney Harbor, with the Opera House and Harbor Bridge, is one of Australia's best-known landmarks.

by people who were originally of many nationalities – not just from Europe but from countries around the world.

Today Australia has a developed economy. Agriculture is important. There is a great range of farms, from small, specialist vineyards producing famous Australian wines, to massive ranches where cattle and sheep are reared. Industry is varied but is particularly focused on primary production – mining raw materials, for example.

Due to its size and location, Australia has one of the most diverse ranges of environments on Earth, including deserts, tropical rain forests, and snowcapped mountains. There are other important variations within the country, too – such as where people live, the distribution of large cities, and how easy it is to get around by public transportation.

AUSTRALIA AT A GLANCE

- Area: 2,968,125 square miles (7,686,850 sq km)
- Population (1993 estimate): 17,827,204
- Population density: 6 people per sq mi (2.3 people per sq km)
- Capital: Canberra, population 310,000 (1990)
- Other main cities: Sydney 3.6 million; Melbourne 3.1 million; Brisbane 1.3 million; Perth 1.2 million; Adelaide 1.05 million
- Highest mountain: Mount Kosciusko, 7,310 feet (2,228 m)
- Longest river: Darling, 1,702 miles (2,739 km)
- Language: English
- Major religion: Christianity
- Life expectancy: 73.3 years for men; 79.9 for women
- Currency: Australian dollar, written as $A ($A 1 = 100 cents)
- Economy: CAPITALIST economy, based on agriculture and minerals
- Major resources: A wide range of minerals, including bauxite, coal, iron ore, copper, tin, silver, and uranium
- Major exports: Meat, wool, wheat, machinery and transportation equipment, alumina, gold, coal
- Environmental problems: Destruction of good-quality soil (for example, through poor agricultural management), SALINIZATION, DESERTIFICATION, CYCLONES along the northern coast, fresh water availability, droughts, bushfires

THE LANDSCAPE

Australia has three main landscape subdivisions: the Western Plateau; the Interior Lowlands, or Central Plains; and the Eastern Highlands, or Great Dividing Range.

The Western Plateau covers about half the continent and is flat, barren land extending more than 1,115 miles (1,800 km) from west to east. Most of it is desert. Not all the deserts have sand dunes. Some have gently rolling surfaces strewn with rocks and boulders. In the south is the Nullabor Plain, a flat, barren, limestone lowland riddled by underground caves. Much of the Western Plateau is termed the OUTBACK because of its remoteness.

KEY FACTS

● Australia covers 5.2% of the land surface of the world.
● Australia is the smallest continent and the sixth largest country.
● It is slightly smaller than the U.S., half the size of Europe and less than one-fifth the size of Asia.
● Desert and semidesert cover about two-thirds of the country.
● Australia has 16,007 miles (25,760 km) of coastline.

▲ Uluru (Ayers Rock) in Northern Territory, one of the oldest rocks on Earth.

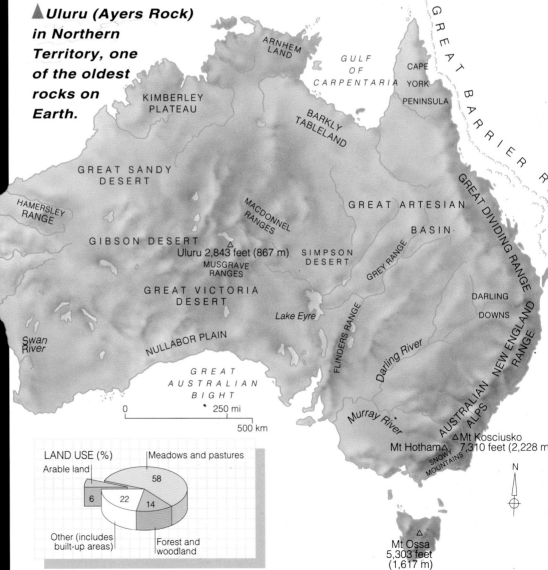

ARNHEM LAND

GULF OF CARPENTARIA

CAPE YORK PENINSULA

GREAT BARRIER R

KIMBERLEY PLATEAU

BARKLY TABLELAND

GREAT SANDY DESERT

HAMERSLEY RANGE

MACDONNEL RANGES

GREAT ARTESIAN BASIN

GREAT DIVIDING RANGE

GIBSON DESERT

Uluru 2,843 feet (867 m)
MUSGRAVE RANGES

SIMPSON DESERT

GREY RANGE

GREAT VICTORIA DESERT

Lake Eyre

FLINDERS RANGE

DARLING DOWNS

Swan River

NULLABOR PLAIN

Darling River

NEW ENGLAND RANGE

GREAT AUSTRALIAN BIGHT

0   250 mi

500 km

Murray River

AUSTRALIAN ALPS

△ Mt Kosciusko
Mt Hotham △ 7,310 feet (2,228 m)
SNOWY MOUNTAINS

N

△ Mt Ossa
5,303 feet (1,617 m)

LAND USE (%)
Arable land   Meadows and pastures

6   22   14   58

Other (includes built-up areas)   Forest and woodland

◀ *The Great Barrier Reef stretches for over 1,180 miles (1,900 km) off the northeast coast.*

▲ *Cross-country skiing on the snow-capped summit of Mount Hotham in the Eastern Highlands.*

The Central Plains are a lowland belt of land reaching south into the fertile area around the Murray-Darling river system, which provides water for 80% of the IRRIGATED farmland in Australia. Beneath the Central Plains are underground water reserves. The biggest reserve is the Great Artesian Basin.

The Eastern Highlands is a 2,230 mile (3,600 km) long mountain range running parallel to the coast, rising to altitudes over 6,500 feet (2,000 m). East of the Range lie 502,000 square miles (1.3 million sq km) of fertile plain. In the north are tropical forests.

Tasmania, the island state off the southeast coast, is an extension of the Eastern Highlands separated from the mainland by the Bass Strait. Tasmania is different from much of the rest of Australia, with lush pastures, rolling hills, and dense forests.

CLIMATE AND WEATHER

Australia's climate has two important characteristics. First, because the country is south of the equator, its seasons are opposite to those in the Northern Hemisphere. Some of the hottest summer temperatures occur in the middle of December. Second, because Australia is such a large country, there are major variations in climate.

Northern Australia is typically tropical, with hot, wet summers and warm winters. Temperatures average around 86°F (30°C) in the summer and 77°F (25°C) in the winter. The summer months there are called "the Wet," because they are so humid. Occasionally at this time there are tropical cyclones — violent storms where winds can reach more than 100 miles (160 km) per hour, and torrential rain can result in extensive flooding. One of the worst of such storms in recent times was Cyclone Tracy, which hit Darwin on Christmas Day 1974. Wind gusts reached 150 mph (240 kph). About 50 people were killed and

▲ *Warm temperatures in December, January, and February encourage outdoor activities. Bondi Beach near Sydney is especially popular, and many people visit it for a swim or a beach party on Christmas Day.*

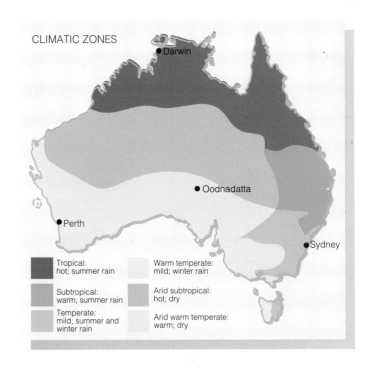

CLIMATIC ZONES

Darwin

Oodnadatta

Perth

Sydney

Tropical:
hot; summer rain

Subtropical:
warm; summer rain

Temperate:
mild; summer and
winter rain

Warm temperate:
mild; winter rain

Arid subtropical:
hot; dry

Arid warm temperate:
warm; dry

KEY FACTS

● Nearly 40% of Australia lies between the Tropic of Capricorn and the Equator.
● Over a third of Australia receives less than 10.4 in (260 mm) of rainfall each year.
● On an average day Australia has over 8 hours of sunshine.
● The hottest months are January and February in southern Australia, but November and December in the north.
● The Alice Springs area has an average of 10.8 dust storms a year.
● In Whim Creek in Western Australia, 30 in (745 mm) of rain fell in a single day in January 1986, but only 0.17 in (4.3 mm) fell in the whole of 1924.

others were reported missing at sea.

Much of Australia is arid. Temperatures are hot and there is little rain. A good example is Alice Springs in the Northern Territory, where summer temperatures frequently exceed 95°F (35°C). Rainfall is extremely variable and is seldom more than 8 in (200 mm) per year. Even if rain does fall, the dry heat means that much of it evaporates. Because of the dry conditions, a large part of Australia's interior is classed as desert. Dust storms are common and are often a major problem in towns and cities.

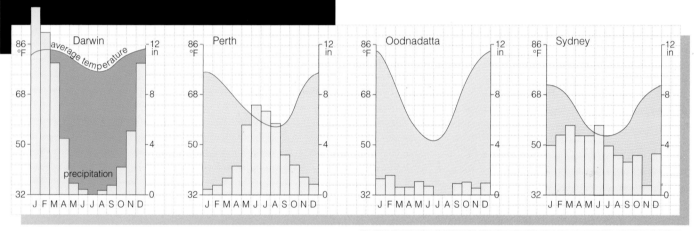

▲ There are variations in temperatures and rainfall throughout Australia. For example, some places have more rain in the summer, others have more in the winter.

◀ Australia's size and location mean there is a wide variety of climatic zones, from typically tropical areas to dry regions.

▶ Rainfall distribution highlights the dryness of the interior, with a rapid decline in rainfall away from coastal locations.

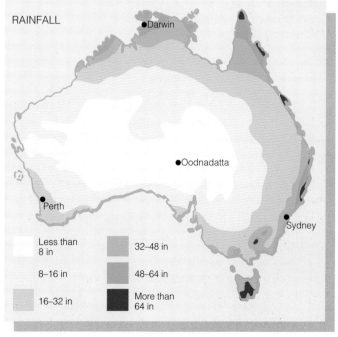

They can reduce visibility to less than 330 feet (100 m) at times.

Because of the lack of rainfall, many of Australia's rivers do not flow into the sea but meet around Lake Eyre, some 43 feet (13 m) below sea level. Throughout much of the year this lake is a zone of dry, salt-encrusted mud with scattered water holes known as BILLABONGS.

Because Australia is a country that has many hours of sunshine throughout the year, skin cancer is a major problem. People sunbathe or walk around without protecting themselves from the effects of exposure to the sun's harmful rays. There have been big attempts recently to reduce the incidence of skin cancer through advertising campaigns and television commercials, especially using the phrase "slip, slop, slap" – meaning "slip on a

▶ *A dried-out lake at Menindee, New South Wales.*

▼ *While some northern areas seldom suffer a lack of water, other regions are often subject to droughts.*

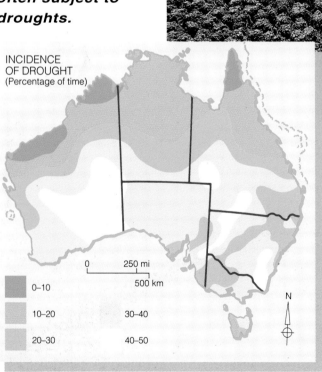

INCIDENCE
OF DROUGHT
(Percentage of time)

0   250 mi

500 km

0–10	
10–20	30–40
20–30	40–50

N

▶ **The Russell Falls in the state of Tasmania, lush with green vegetation, reflect the cooler, damper conditions on the island. This is in stark contrast to the deserts of the interior, where riverbeds are usually dry and vegetation is virtually absent.**

T-shirt, slop on some sun lotion, and slap on a hat."

In the far south, Australia has what is called a temperate climate, with conditions similar to those in parts of western Europe. In the island state of Tasmania, for example, summers are mild but in winter temperatures often drop below freezing and snow can fall.

One other interesting variation occurs along the eastern edge of the country, due to a chain of mountains. The altitude of the Snowy Mountains, Australian Alps, and South-Eastern Highlands means there is more regular rainfall and snow. This is because moist air blows in from the Tasman Sea and is forced up over the mountains. As the moist air rises, it cools. The water vapor in the air condenses to form clouds and rain falls.

Australia produces 80 commercially significant minerals, including bauxite, coal, iron ore, uranium, natural gas, and petroleum. Some of the reserves are massive. For instance, the Mount Goldsworthy iron ore mine in Western Australia is estimated to contain over 15 billion tons. In New South Wales the silver, lead, and zinc deposits of the Broken Hill mining province have already yielded over 147 million tons of ore. New mineral deposits are still being found, such as the copper deposit at Roxby Downs.

The economy of many towns in the outback is based on the mining industry. For example, Kalgoorlie in Western Australia developed because of gold mining, and Coober Pedy in South Australia as a result of mining opals.

Australia has large energy resources too. Some 70% of the country's petroleum requirement is met from national reserves,

◀ *The iron ore mine at Koolan Island, Western Australia, is slowly removing the side of a hill. The building and vehicles in the foreground are tiny compared with the massive excavation.*

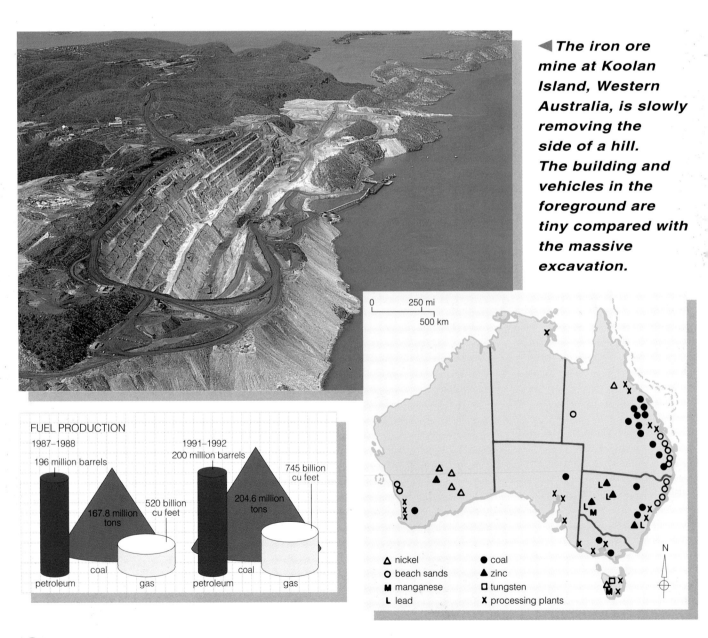

FUEL PRODUCTION

1987–1988
196 million barrels
167.8 million tons
520 billion cu feet
petroleum coal gas

1991–1992
200 million barrels
204.6 million tons
745 billion cu feet
petroleum coal gas

0   250 mi
500 km

△ nickel   ● coal
○ beach sands   ▲ zinc
M manganese   □ tungsten
L lead   X processing plants

N

while coal, which is important in generating electricity, is produced in several Australian states.

Forestry products form another key resource. In Tasmania, areas of woodland provide several wood products, including wood chips from native eucalyptus forests, which are exported.

Because much of Australia is very dry, there are some major water management plans. Some relate to the GROUNDWATER

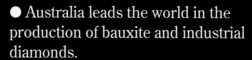
reserves of the Great Artesian Basin in the southeast. Others involve the collection and storage of water in the Eastern Highlands. The Snowy Mountains plan in the Eastern Alps has 16 major dams, 7 power stations, and many miles of tunnels and aqueducts. The project took 23 years to complete and cost $A 800 million. It opened in 1972.

▲ *Opal mining activities at Coober Pedy, South Australia, have produced piles of waste that look like the craters of a "moonscape."*

▶ *Windmills are used to pump water from large natural underground reservoirs.*

LEADING PRODUCERS OF GOLD AND SILVER, 1992 (tons)

GOLD
South Africa 608.5
U.S. 296
Australia 240

SILVER
Mexico 2,325
U.S. 1,741
Peru 1,595.2
Australia 1,248

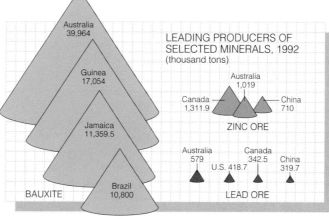

BAUXITE
Australia 39,964
Guinea 17,054
Jamaica 11,359.5
Brazil 10,800

LEADING PRODUCERS OF SELECTED MINERALS, 1992 (thousand tons)

ZINC ORE
Australia 1,019
Canada 1,311.9
China 710

LEAD ORE
Australia 579
U.S. 418.7
Canada 342.5
China 319.7

POPULATION

More than 85% of Australia's people live in towns and cities. About two-thirds live in Sydney, Melbourne, Brisbane, Adelaide, and Perth — each of which has over 1 million inhabitants. Most of the large cities are in the eastern part of the country, in New South Wales, Victoria, and Queensland. Perth is the one exception, being located on the west coast of Western Australia. Many people also live close to the coast. There is an almost total absence of people in the center of Australia and large areas of land are completely uninhabited.

The white population is mostly of European origin. Over 70% have European ancestors and nearly 40% have relatives in the United Kingdom or Ireland. There is a high proportion of young people compared with other countries, partly due to the high birthrate after World War II and partly due to the high number of immigrants. Over 70% of Australians are less than 45 years

► *Flinders Street Station in Melbourne, Victoria, at the heart of one of Australia's largest cities. Trolleys or streetcars are a popular means of public transportation in the city.*

▼ *A lone homestead at Silverton in the New South Wales outback. Much of the interior is sparsely populated, and neighbors can live many miles away.*

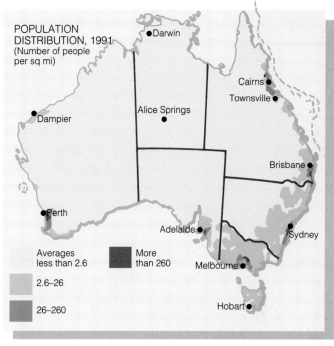

POPULATION
DISTRIBUTION, 1991
(Number of people
per sq mi)

Darwin

Cairns

Townsville

Dampier

Alice Springs

Brisbane

Perth

Adelaide

Sydney

| Averages | More |
| less than 2.6 | than 260 |

Melbourne

2.6–26

Hobart

26–260

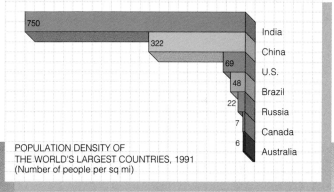

750	India
322	China
69	U.S.
48	Brazil
22	Russia
7	Canada
6	Australia

POPULATION DENSITY OF
THE WORLD'S LARGEST COUNTRIES, 1991
(Number of people per sq mi)

◀An Aboriginal corroboree. The long piece of carved wood is a DIDGERIDOO, an Aboriginal musical instrument.

▼Recent immigrants have arrived from a wide range of countries. Like other Australians, most live in towns or cities.

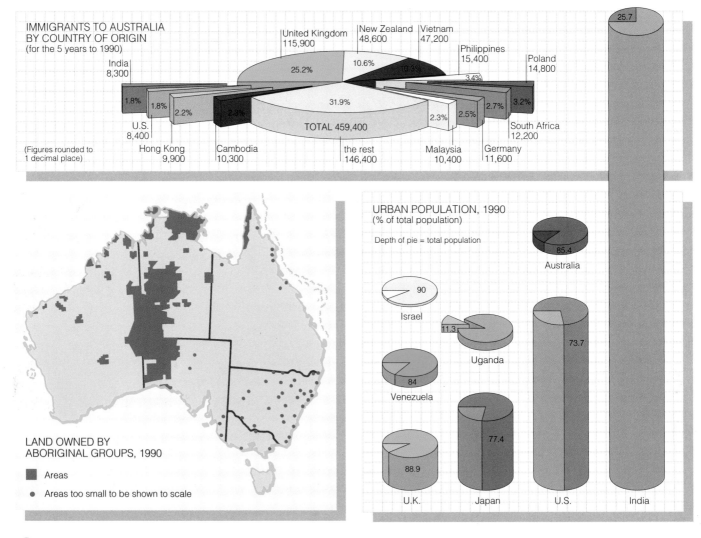

IMMIGRANTS TO AUSTRALIA
BY COUNTRY OF ORIGIN
(for the 5 years to 1990)

United Kingdom 115,900 — 25.2%
New Zealand 48,600 — 10.6%
Vietnam 47,200 — 10.3%
Philippines 15,400 — 3.4%
Poland 14,800 — 3.2%
South Africa 12,200 — 2.7%
Germany 11,600 — 2.5%
Malaysia 10,400 — 2.3%
the rest 146,400 — 31.9%
Cambodia 10,300 — 2.3%
Hong Kong 9,900 — 2.2%
U.S. 8,400 — 1.8%
India 8,300 — 1.8%

TOTAL 459,400

(Figures rounded to 1 decimal place)

LAND OWNED BY
ABORIGINAL GROUPS, 1990

■ Areas

● Areas too small to be shown to scale

URBAN POPULATION, 1990
(% of total population)

Depth of pie = total population

Israel 90
Australia 85.4
Uganda 11.3
Venezuela 84
U.K. 88.9
Japan 77.4
U.S. 73.7
India 25.7

of age (1993 estimate) and almost a quarter are under 14 years old.

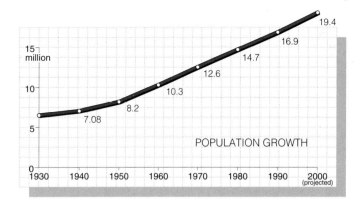

POPULATION GROWTH

The pattern of immigration has changed in recent years. After World War II, greater numbers of immigrants arrived from southern European countries, such as Greece and Italy. Today a significant proportion of all new arrivals in Australia are from Asian countries, such as Malaysia, Hong Kong, Brunei, and Singapore. Recent immigrants have included refugees from Vietnam, Laos, and Cambodia. Asian immigrants tend to cluster together in large cities. Many have brought important skills in industry and business which have helped the Australian economy.

The original inhabitants of Australia are the Aborigines. Although they were originally rural, nomadic people, today more than 60% live in urban areas. They form only about 1.5% of the country's population, compared with a white population of about 95% and an Asian total of 4%. Aborigines have a strong culture and sense of identity and pride. An

important idea is "Dreamtime," which represents the Aboriginal cultural, historical, and ancestral heritage. They believe that Dreamtime was the dawn of all creation when the land, the rivers, rain, wind, and all living things were generated. It is also the Aboriginal way of linking the past, present, and future. Large groups of Aborigines meet periodically to hold a "corroboree," a ceremony where songs and dances are used in celebrations. During these gatherings, the men decorate their bodies with white paint made from soil and crushed rocks.

KEY FACTS

● There are 317.2 people per sq mi (122.6 per sq km) in the Australian Capital Territory, compared with only 0.26 (0.1) in Northern Territory.
● Each day in Australia approximately 700 babies are born and 360 people die.
● Today there are about 238,600 Aborigines in Australia, compared with an estimated 750,000 when Europeans arrived in 1788.
● Between June 1991 and June 1992, a total of 107,390 people arrived in Australia to settle permanently.

▲*The Vietnamese community in Cabramatta, Sydney, developed as a result of immigration from Southeast Asia.*

DAILY LIFE

RELIGION

More than 84% of Australians belong to a religious denomination. The majority are Christian, either Protestant or Roman Catholic, reflecting the early settlers who arrived from Europe in the late 18th and 19th centuries. With the increasing number of immigrants from Southeast Asia, other religions, such as Islam and Buddhism, are now growing rapidly.

EDUCATION

Literacy rates are generally high, although the Aborigines have suffered disadvantages and many cannot read or write. The school year runs from February to mid-December, and education is free up to university level. Children start primary school at the age of 5 or 6 and leave at 12. Secondary education is compulsory up to the age of 15 (16 in Tasmania). School students work toward important examinations that are taken at 15 and 17 years of age. Those taken at the age of 17 are known as the Higher School Certificate, which students must pass if they

▲ *Farmers in the outback often use motorbikes rather than horses to cover the large distances between their herds of livestock.*

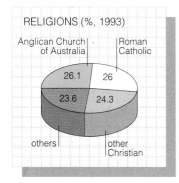

RELIGIONS (%, 1993)

Anglican Church of Australia | Roman Catholic

26.1 | 26

23.6 | 24.3

others | other Christian

▲ *Most Australians are Christians, although other religions are growing.*

want to go on to a public university.

Unique to Australia are Schools of the Air, designed to reach children who live in remote areas. Children talk to teachers during lessons using two-way radios. The first such school was set up in Alice Springs in 1951.

HEALTH

Australia's health system, known as Medicare, is open to everyone and guarantees medical and eye care. A famous part of the medical service is the Royal Flying Doctor Service, established in 1927, which allows doctors to fly in small planes to visit patients. The planes are also used as air ambulances. The RFDS operates a radio service so that people in remote areas can seek medical advice and find out what to do if someone is ill or injured.

SPORTS AND LEISURE

Sports are an everyday part of Australian life. Famous teams include the Wallabies, the national rugby union squad. Australia is also

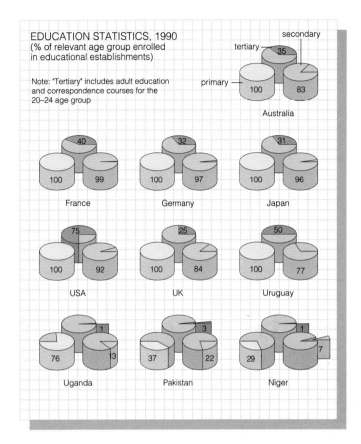

EDUCATION STATISTICS, 1990
(% of relevant age group enrolled in educational establishments)

Note: "Tertiary" includes adult education and correspondence courses for the 20–24 age group

secondary
tertiary — 35
primary — 100   83

Australia

France   40   100   99

Germany   32   100   97

Japan   31   100   96

USA   75   100   92

UK   25   100   84

Uruguay   50   100   77

Uganda   76   1   3

Pakistan   37   3   22

Niger   29   1   7

▼ *These children in Western Australia are members of the School of the Air. They work at home and talk to their teacher over a two-way radio.*

◀ *Many people in Coober Pedy, South Australia, live in caves hewn out of rock. The underground homes provide excellent shelter from the high temperatures and burning sun.*

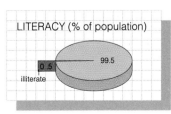

LITERACY (% of population)

0.5
illiterate   99.5

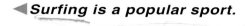

◀ *Surfing is a popular sport.*

▼ *Australian Rules Football was developed in Melbourne in the mid-19th century. A match is divided into 4 quarters of 25 minutes.*

FESTIVALS AND HOLIDAYS

January 1	New Year's Day
January 26	Australia Day (celebrates the founding of the colony of New South Wales on January 26, 1788)
March or April	Easter
April 25	Anzac Day (commemorates the landing of Australian and New Zealand forces at Gallipoli in 1915 in World War I)
Early June	The Queen's Birthday
Early October	Labor Day
December 25	Christmas Day
December 26	Boxing Day

▶ *Spare-time activities often include water sports such as waterskiing and windsurfing. These boats in Sydney Harbor are participating in the Tall Ships Race, held as part of Australia's Bicentenary celebrations in 1988.*

well known for its cricket and its Australian Rules Football. This is a mixture of Gaelic football, soccer, and rugby, played with an oval ball, on an oval field, with 18 players per team. Play consists mostly of kicking or punching the ball. The Grand Final of the Australian Rules Football season is every bit as important in Australia as the final game of the Super Bowl in the United States.

Many sports are associated with Australians' love for the beach and sea. There are frequent surf carnivals in the summer at places like Bondi Beach near Sydney. Yacht teams compete for the Davis Cup, which is awarded to the winning crew of the Sydney to Hobart yacht race. Other activities include swimming, shooting, horse racing, canoeing, skiing, camping, and bush-walking. Occasionally Australians will "go bush," meaning to get away from the stress of urban living for a while by trekking in the outback.

KEY FACTS

● In 1991, a total of 3,075,137 children were enrolled in primary and secondary schools.
● The average distance between classmates in the Carnarvon School of the Air, Western Australia, is 25 miles (42 km).
● In 1986 there were 1,072 hospitals in Australia and 1 doctor for every 552 people (compared with 1 for every 650 people in the UK and 1 for every 419 in the U.S.).
● The average life expectancy of Aborigines is 15–20 years less than the national average.
● The standard working week is 38 hours long.
● The average Australian household contains 2.9 people.

▶ *These Aborigines are painting designs using natural products. The designs are often handed down from generation to generation and form part of Aboriginal culture. Many of the shapes have important meanings related to traditional lifestyles.*

Australia has a Federal Parliament with representatives from the six states, two territories, and a number of dependent areas, such as Christmas Island. Its system is similar to that in the United Kingdom, although members of both Houses of Parliament are elected. There are 147 seats in the House of Representatives and 76 in the Senate. Elections are held every three years. The head of the political party that wins the most seats becomes prime minister. In a similar manner to Great Britain, Queen Elizabeth II is head of state. She is represented in Australia by the governor-general.

The federal government, based in Canberra, occupies the Australian Capital Territory (ACT). It is responsible for matters such as defense, foreign policy, national economic policy, and immigration.

Each state and territory has its own

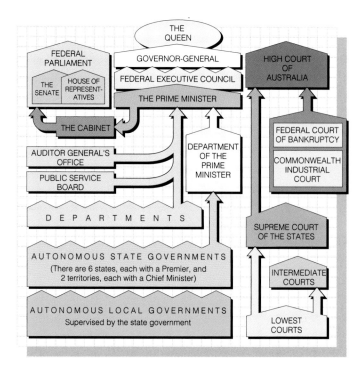

▼ **An Anzac Day ceremony in Canberra, Australia's capital city. Federal government buildings can be seen in the distance.**

KEY FACTS

● After Europeans arrived in 1788, Australia was governed from Great Britain.

● Transportation of convicts ended in 1868.

● Australia achieved independence on January 1, 1901.

● Voting is compulsory at the age of 18. People who do not vote can be fined.

● In ACT about 60% of the workforce is employed by the government.

● There is one police officer in Australia for approximately every 550 people.

● Some government areas are very large – Northern Territory is 2.5 times the size of France and 6 times the size of Britain.

● As of June 1993, there were 63,200 personnel in Australia's armed forces – 28,600 in the army, 19,300 in the air force and 15,300 in the navy.

▲ *Protests about the rights of Aboriginal people, or "Kooris," have been a feature of recent years.*

government and legal systems. The head of government in a state is called the premier and in a territory the chief minister. State government responsibilities include education, housing, health, the welfare of Aborigines, tourism, and natural resources.

Law enforcement is divided between federal and state governments. The Australian Federal Police deals with matters like drugs, government crime, and terrorism. Each state also has its own police force that is responsible for law enforcement at the local level.

◀ *The seven-pointed Commonwealth star on the Australian flag represents the country's states and territories. The other stars represent the Southern Cross constellation.*

FOOD AND FARMING

Because of Australia's diverse climate and soil conditions, there is a vast range of crops in the country. Cereal crops are grown over wide areas in all states and territories, whereas other crops are confined to specific locations. Chief items are wheat, barley, sugarcane, and fruit such as papaws, mangoes, currants, grapes, strawberries, oranges, and apples. Industrial crops include cotton, flax, and peanuts. Wine is produced in vineyards, especially in the Hunter Valley and Barossa Valley.

The main wheat-growing areas extend in a belt west of the Great Dividing Range from New South Wales into Victoria and across the southern part of South Australia. There is

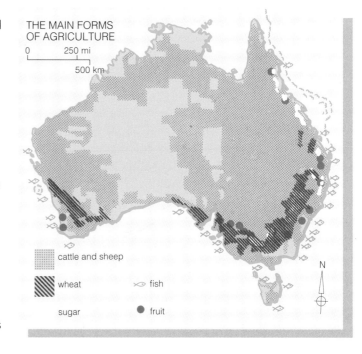

THE MAIN FORMS OF AGRICULTURE

0   250 mi

500 km

cattle and sheep

wheat   fish

sugar   fruit

N

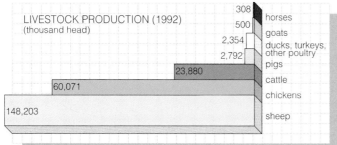

LIVESTOCK PRODUCTION (1992)
(thousand head)

308	horses
500	goats
2,354	ducks, turkeys, other poultry
2,792	pigs
23,880	cattle
60,071	chickens
148,203	sheep

▼ *There are more sheep in Australia than in any other country in the world, and the majority are in the southeast of the country. They are reared for both wool and meat.*

▲ **Sugarcane farms in Australia are regarded as among the most mechanized in the world.**

10,450		wool
10,450		beef
7,150		wheat
3,850		sugar
2,750		raw cotton
2,200		barley
1,650		lamb/mutton

MAJOR AGRICULTURAL
EXPORTS BY VALUE (1992)
($A thousands)

KEY FACTS

● Only 2% of the land available for crops in Australia is cultivated.

● Although two-thirds of Australia is used for livestock farming, much of the land is dry and of poor quality.

● There are around 180,000 farms in Australia, covering a total of 1,206 million acres (482.5 million ha).

● Australia produces about 30% of the world's total wool supply.

● Australia is the world's 4th largest exporter of wheat.

● Australia is the world's 6th largest beef- and veal-producing nation.

● Of all the mutton exported from Australia, almost 61% goes to Saudi Arabia and Kuwait.

● The merino sheep breed was first introduced to Australia in 1797.

● The most important state for sheep-rearing is New South Wales.

● Almost 25% of Australia's cattle are dairy breeds.

● About half of the country's cattle are reared in the state of Victoria.

● The average consumption of beer per person in 1986 was 36.4 gallons (140 liters), compared with 19 gallons (73.9 liters) of soft drinks, and 3.5 gallons (13.5 liters) of tea.

◄ **Cowboys, or "stockmen," look after the cattle and maintain the fences on cattle stations.**

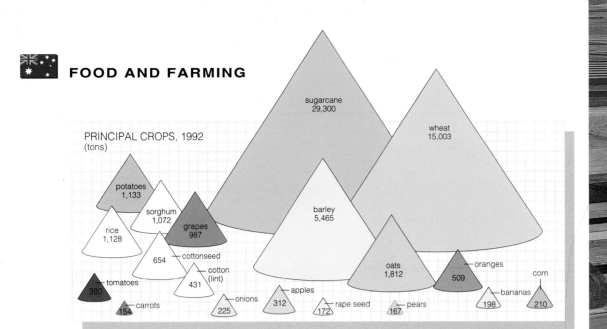

PRINCIPAL CROPS, 1992
(tons)

sugarcane
29,300

wheat
15,003

potatoes
1,133

sorghum
1,072

grapes
987

rice
1,128

654 — cottonseed

cotton
(lint)
431

tomatoes
380

carrots
154

onions
225

barley
5,465

apples
312

rape seed
172

pears
167

oats
1,812

509

oranges

bananas
198

corn
210

DAILY FOOD SUPPLY,1990 (calories/grams of protein per inhabitant)

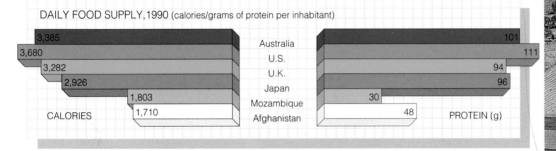

	CALORIES		PROTEIN (g)
Australia	3,385		101
U.S.	3,680		111
U.K.	3,282		94
Japan	2,926		96
Mozambique	1,803		30
Afghanistan	1,710		48

▼ **An Aboriginal child in Northern Territory about to eat a wichety grub. Other traditional foods include daisy yams and turtle eggs.**

► **The green rolling fields of the Darling Downs in Queensland. This is one of Australia's most agriculturally productive areas.**

also an extensive area in southwest Western Australia. Wheat yields vary greatly from year to year because of erratic rainfall. The main barley-growing areas are in South Australia, while oats are grown in the south where rainfall is fairly uniform. Almost 95% of Australia's rice production is concentrated in New South Wales and 95% of sugarcane production is in Queensland because of the warm, tropical climate. Many farms are highly mechanized.

The principal livestock are cattle, sheep, and poultry. Some cattle and sheep farms

cover thousands of square miles in the outback. They are called "stations." Dairying flourishes in the eastern and southeastern coastal areas and inland on the Darling Downs of Queensland. Beef cattle are more widespread. About 75% of Australia's wool production is from the merino sheep breed.

Mullett, tuna, and snoek are all caught in near-shore coastal waters. Grayling, prawns, oysters, and scallops are also fished, largely for sale in Japan and the United States.

Traditionally, Australians' main meal includes meat, vegetables, and a dessert, which might be a PAVLOVA, regarded as a national dish, or a Lamington – a sponge cake covered with chocolate and coconut. Kangaroo and crocodile meat are served in many restaurants. Today there is also a wealth of foreign foods, partly because of immigrants arriving from Asian countries. Cantonese, Japanese, Indonesian, Thai, Vietnamese, and Korean foods are all popular.

The Aborigines traditionally eat from the land. Although their diet today is very westernized, many still know which berries are juicy and which plants are edible.

TRADE AND INDUSTRY

Industry employs about 30% of the Australian workforce. Due to the abundance of natural resources, the country is a major exporter of agricultural products, minerals, and fossil fuels, including coal, oil, and natural gas.

MANUFACTURING

The manufacturing industry has been expanding rapidly, particularly since the end of World War II. In 1989–90 the country had 41,797 registered companies, employing a total of over 1 million people. Manufacturing is concentrated around the east coast, with the main centers in Sydney, Adelaide, Melbourne, and Brisbane. Important industries are shipbuilding, car construction, metals, textiles, clothing, food processing, and wine.

Some cities are especially important for certain products. For example, Sydney is

▲ *Assembling Mitsubishi cars at the Tonsley Park Manufacturing Center in Adelaide. At this point on the assembly line, the car engine is being matched to the bodywork.*

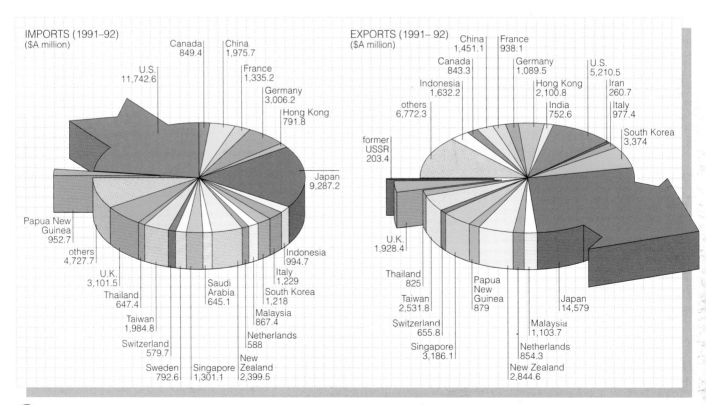

IMPORTS (1991–92) ($A million)

Canada 849.4
China 1,975.7
U.S. 11,742.6
France 1,335.2
Germany 3,006.2
Hong Kong 791.8
Japan 9,287.2
Papua New Guinea 952.7
others 4,727.7
Indonesia 994.7
U.K. 3,101.5
Italy 1,229
Saudi Arabia 645.1
South Korea 1,218
Thailand 647.4
Malaysia 867.4
Taiwan 1,984.8
Netherlands 588
Switzerland 579.7
New Zealand 2,399.5
Sweden 792.6
Singapore 1,301.1

EXPORTS (1991–92) ($A million)

China 1,451.1
France 938.1
Canada 843.3
Germany 1,089.5
U.S. 5,210.5
Indonesia 1,632.2
Hong Kong 2,100.8
Iran 260.7
others 6,772.3
India 752.6
Italy 977.4
former USSR 203.4
South Korea 3,374
U.K. 1,928.4
Thailand 825
Papua New Guinea 879
Japan 14,579
Taiwan 2,531.8
Switzerland 655.8
Malaysia 1,103.7
Singapore 3,186.1
Netherlands 854.3
New Zealand 2,844.6

noted for the production of transportation equipment; Hobart for textiles, clothing, and footwear; Shepparton for food, beverages, and tobacco. Australia's manufacturing output is weak compared with many other developed countries, because many industries developed late compared with other nations.

OVERSEAS TRADE

Australia has a relatively small domestic market, in part due to its low population, so trade with other countries is important. The cost of shipping manufactured goods abroad over large distances means that transportation expenses are high.

Principal exports include coal, gold, meat, wool, alumina, wheat, and machinery. Of Australia's top 25 exports, 21 are raw materials — known as primary products. Chief imports include computer and office machinery, transportation equipment, crude oil, and petroleum products.

In the past, trade with foreign countries was focused on countries in the West, such as the U.S. and those in Europe, because of historical links. Today, however, trade with countries in the Pacific region is increasingly important. These are called the Pacific Rim countries, as many of them lie around the edge of the Pacific Ocean. Two-thirds of

LARGEST IMPORTS IN 1991–92 ($A million)

2,556	road vehicles
2,168	aircraft and associated equipment
1,924	office and automatic data processing machines
1,577	gasoline and oils

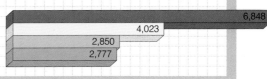

LARGEST EXPORTS IN 1991–92 ($A million)

coal	6,848
gold	4,023
iron ore concentrates	2,850
meat of bovine animals	2,777

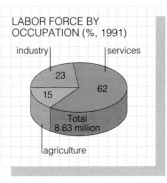

LABOR FORCE BY OCCUPATION (%, 1991)

industry 23
services 62
agriculture 15
Total 8.63 million

◀ *Gladstone Power Station in Queensland is a major supplier of electricity to both domestic and industrial consumers.*

▲ *Surfers Paradise, Queensland, is one of the most popular resorts both for Australians and for foreign tourists. Numerous high-rise hotels fringe the long beach there.*

Australia's trade is now with Pacific Rim countries. Britain was once Australia's main trading partner, but this changed when the U.K. joined the European Community (now the European Union). Its place has been taken by Japan, with the U.S. a close second, followed by New Zealand, South Korea, and Singapore. Nearly a quarter of all goods entering Australia from abroad comes from the United States, followed by

Japan at 19% and Great Britain at 6%.

One of the major concerns for trade abroad centers on barriers or rules made by other countries that work against free trade for Australian companies. Trade barriers make exporting difficult, because the goods become too expensive for people to buy. The Australian government has been working hard to overcome these obstacles. For instance, agreements have been signed that secure closer economic ties with New Zealand, to eliminate trade barriers and to promote the exchange of goods between the two countries.

▶ **At Shark Bay, Western Australia, dolphins swim right up to the rangers to be fed. Visitors get close-up views of these animals, which normally live deep in the ocean.**

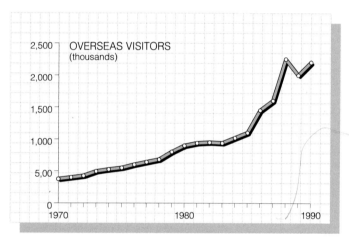

OVERSEAS VISITORS (thousands)

2,500
2,000
1,500
1,000
5,00
0

1970   1980   1990

KEY FACTS

● In 1991–92, almost 2.4 million people visited Australia.
● Tourism provides 40,000 jobs.
● Wage rates in Australia are among the highest in the world.
● Unemployment rates among Aborigines are more than 6 times greater than the national average.

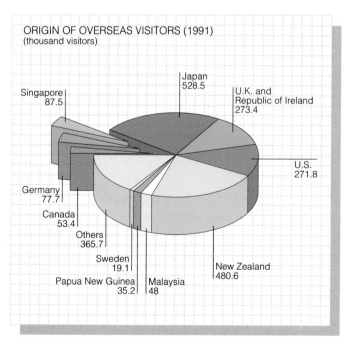

ORIGIN OF OVERSEAS VISITORS (1991)
(thousand visitors)

Singapore 87.5
Germany 77.7
Canada 53.4
Others 365.7
Sweden 19.1
Papua New Guinea 35.2
Malaysia 48
New Zealand 480.6
Japan 528.5
U.K. and Republic of Ireland 273.4
U.S. 271.8

TOURISM

Tourism is the fastest growing part of the Australian economy today and presently employs over 40,000 people. It has been promoted by films like *Crocodile Dundee* and events such as the Australian Bicentennial celebrations in 1988. Big tourist attractions include the Sydney Opera House and Harbor Bridge, Uluru or Ayers Rock, the Great Barrier Reef, and animals such as kangaroos, koalas, and frilled-neck lizards. Overseas visitors spend more than $A 2.5 billion in Australia each year.

TRANSPORTATION

Australia has an extensive road and rail network, but many routes are confined to coastal locations and link the major port cities. Because transportation is the responsibility of individual states, the width of railroad track may change between one state and another.

Over much of Australia, low population densities mean that good quality roads are few and far between. There is a high rate of traffic accidents and deaths, despite the compulsory wearing of seat belts. Traffic in towns and cities can be highly congested, due to the reliance on private cars.

Australia has 439 usable airports. Of these, 69 are owned by government authorities and 370 are owned privately. Qantas, the national airline, initiated the first round-the-world air service in 1958. Qantas stands for "Queensland and Northern Territory Aerial Service." The company flies to 40 cities in 24 countries around the world.

There are 12 major ports and 70 smaller

▲ *The Indian Pacific train, which runs between Perth and Sydney, seen here crossing the Nullabor Plain in Western Australia.*

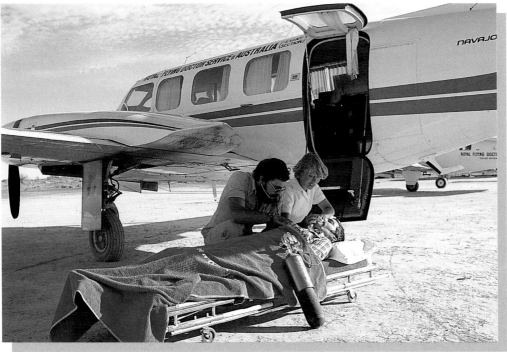

◄ *A patient being treated by a member of the Royal Flying Doctor Service, which serves the outback.*

▶ *Goods are often moved by* ROAD TRAIN, *a series of linked trucks (called dogs) which travel at high speed. A road train can transport over 1,000 sheep or several hundred cattle at one time. This one is carrying fuel.*

harbors where goods can be loaded and unloaded. The most important ports are Dampier, Port Hedland, Newcastle, Hay Point, and Sydney. Australia has a poor selection of natural harbors and several large ports require continuous dredging to remove silt and mud. There are only 5,196.7 miles (8,363 km) of inland waterways, because of the seasonal nature of the rivers.

KEY FACTS

● The distance from London to Sydney by air is 10,565 miles (17,003 km). From Los Angeles to Sydney it is 7,449 miles (11,988 km).

● The Indian Pacific train covers 2,456 miles (3,955 km) between Perth and Sydney and includes the longest stretch of straight track in the world.

● There are around 10 million motor vehicles in Australia.

● Most of the public railroads are within 180 miles (300 km) of the coast.

● In 1993, Australia had 22,050 miles (35,486 km) of railroads, compared with 23,296 miles (37,491 km) in the U.K. (which is almost 16 times smaller).

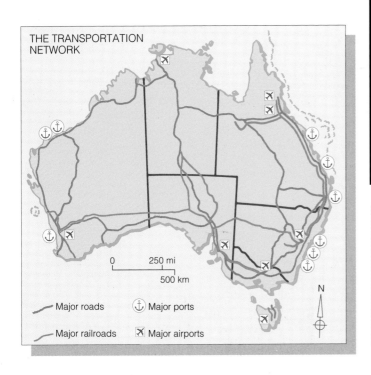

THE TRANSPORTATION NETWORK

0 — 250 mi
— 500 km

N

— Major roads

⚓ Major ports

— Major railroads

☒ Major airports

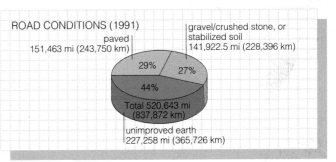

ROAD CONDITIONS (1991)

paved
151,463 mi (243,750 km)

gravel/crushed stone, or stabilized soil
141,922.5 mi (228,396 km)

29%

27%

44%

Total 520,643 mi (837,872 km)

unimproved earth
227,258 mi (365,726 km)

THE ENVIRONMENT

The range of Australian environments is diverse, varying from dry, sandy deserts in the center to tropical rain forests in the north, to cool, temperate woodlands in Tasmania.

Many of Australia's plants and animals are in danger of becoming extinct because their natural habitats are under threat. This is partly because of exploitation by humans, partly because of the introduction of foreign plants and animals, and in some places because of chemical pollution. Endangered species include the hairy-nosed wombat, ghost bat, western swamp turtle, paradise parrot, and swamp orchid.

National parks and nature preserves include Uluru National Park in Northern Territory and the Great Barrier Reef Marine Park in Queensland. The Australian Heritage Commission is responsible for looking after places of important environmental significance. The commission keeps a register that lists 8,000 important sites, including national parks and Aboriginal sites. The Aboriginal sites are particularly important, because of their cultural significance and because they are many centuries old.

A major environmental problem in Australia is overgrazing caused by large numbers of cattle and sheep. In many

▼ *Bushfires raging in Kakadu National Park. Natural fires like this one occur almost every year in Australia and can sweep across thousands of acres.*

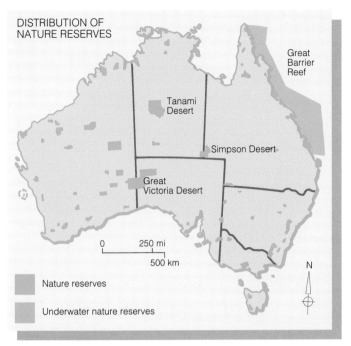

DISTRIBUTION OF
NATURE RESERVES

Great
Barrier
Reef

Tanami
Desert

Simpson Desert

Great
Victoria Desert

0   250 mi

500 km

N

Nature reserves

Underwater nature reserves

parts of the country this has resulted in desertification. The other main soil problem is the buildup of natural salts, due to the excessive use of irrigation water.

Another major environmental hazard is bushfires, the most serious natural hazard in Australia in terms of loss of life over the last 50 years. Devastating examples occurred around Sydney between January 7 and 12, 1994. By the time the fires had been brought under control, four people had been killed and over 200 homes

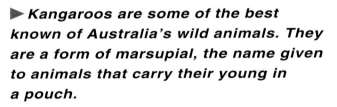

► *Kangaroos are some of the best known of Australia's wild animals. They are a form of marsupial, the name given to animals that carry their young in a pouch.*

▶ *The saltwater crocodile inhabits the* MANGROVE *swamps and marshes of Australia's tropical coastline. This one was photographed in Western Australia.*

destroyed. The total damage was estimated at $A 150 million.

On the positive side, Australia has one of the largest collections of pollution-free, solar-energy generating facilities in the world. It also has some of the most extensive areas of untouched natural beauty on Earth, with many unique species of plants and animals.

▶ *A koala with a baby on her back. Koalas, which feed only on eucalyptus leaves, are one of the traditional symbols of Australia.*

▼ *The Pinnacles Desert, in Western Australia, has been sculpted by the erosion of weak sandstone rocks.*

KEY FACTS

● Australia has some of the world's biggest deserts, including the Simpson, Gibson, and Great Sandy.
● Approximately 107 million acres (43.2 million ha) of grazing are affected by erosion.
● There are 6 World Heritage Sites in Australia, so called because of their outstanding natural beauty and scientific importance.
● About 90% of the state of New South Wales has problems with soil erosion.

⚑■ THE FUTURE

What will the future hold for Australia? Already more people are moving to the big cities and so many smaller outback towns are declining. The population will increase as the birthrate rises. At the same time, people will live longer, putting pressure on crowded residential areas and workplaces.

Australia is also likely to cut its last formal tie to Britain. By the year 2001, the centenary of independence, the country may be a republic with a president as head of state rather than Queen Elizabeth II.

Many farms are inefficient and are being updated. Others will close because of low

▼ *The skyline of Perth in Western Australia, one of the cities that are drawing people to move from rural to urban areas.*

▲ *Queen Elizabeth II, seen here in Western Australia, is head of state. There are suggestions that she may be replaced by a president.*

KEY FACTS

● By 2001 there will be 3 million people over 60 years old, compared with 2 million in 1981.
● Some studies predict that in 2030 Australian temperatures will be between 0.54°F and 4.5°F (0.3° and 2.5°C) higher than their 1990 levels.
● Satellite links are being updated to improve communications, particularly for children who are members of the School of the Air.

▼ *Australia's future lies with its people, a young population of many nationalities living in a country rich in natural resources and potential.*

productivity of overused land. There is a move to conserve the environment more in areas where agriculture is a big money-maker. The future is likely to see an increase in both manufacturing industry and mining activities.

Important changes are taking place to support the Aborigines. In the past they had poor access to housing, hospitals, and schools, for example. This is an increasingly important issue, and recent legislation, known as Mabo, gives Aborigines new rights over places such as Uluru.

The young people of today are regarded as Australia's hope for the future. With careful planning, the country can look forward to a prosperous 21st century as one of the key nations in the southern hemisphere.

FURTHER INFORMATION

● AUSTRALIAN EMBASSY
1601 Massachusetts Avenue N.W.,
Washington, D.C. 20036
● AUSTRALIAN TOURIST COMMISSION
489 Fifth Avenue, New York, N.Y. 10017
● SAN DIEGO ZOOLOGICAL GARDEN
Zoological Society of San Diego
P.O. Box 551, San Diego, CA 92112
● UNITED NATIONS INFORMATION
CENTER
2101 L Street N.W., Washington,
D.C. 20037

BOOKS ABOUT AUSTRALIA

Cobb, Vicki. *This Place Is Lonely*. Walker &
   Co., 1991
Dolce, Laura. *Australia*. Chelsea House, 1990
Garrett, Dan and Grindrod, Warrill. *Australia*,
   "World in View" series. Raintree Steck-
   Vaughn, 1990
Gutnik, Martin J. and Browne-Gutnik,
   Natalie. *Great Barrier Reef*.
   Raintree Steck-Vaughn, 1995
Nile, Richard. *Australian Aborigines*.
   Raintree Steck-Vaughn, 1992
Rajendra, Vijeya. *Australia*. Marshall
   Cavendish, 1991.
Reynolds, J. *Down Under: Vanishing
   Cultures*. HarcourtBrace, 1992
Wilson, Barbara K. *Acacia Terrace*.
   Scholastic Inc., 1990

GLOSSARY

ALUMINA
Concentrated aluminum ore.

BILLABONG
A small water spring.

CAPITALISM
An economic system in which individuals
own businesses and keep the profits.

CYCLONE
A violent storm that usually brings strong
winds and torrential rain.

DESERTIFICATION
The deterioration of land into desert
conditions, due to factors such as lack
of rain, lack of trees, and soil erosion.

DIDGERIDOO
An Aboriginal musical instrument,
consisting of a long, hollow, wooden tube
that produces a low-pitched sound.

GROUNDWATER
Water that is found beneath the surface
of the Earth.

IRRIGATION
The spreading of water across the ground
surface, usually to allow the growing of
crops.

MANGROVE
A type of vegetation that is typical of
tropical swamplands.

OUTBACK
Remote parts of Australia.

PAVLOVA
A type of dessert based on meringue and
cream, often with kiwi fruit.

ROAD TRAIN
A large truck with many trailers used to
transport goods by road.

SALINIZATION
The buildup of natural salts in the soil,
frequently due to irrigation, which makes
the soil infertile.

INDEX

A

Aborigines 8, 20, 21, 22, 25, 27, 30, 31, 35, 38, 43
Adelaide 9, 18, 19, 32
airports 36
Alice Springs 13, 19, 23
animals 38, 40
Australian Alps 15
Ayers Rock *see* Uluru

B

Bass Strait 11
bauxite 9, 17
billabongs 14
Bondi Beach 12, 25
Brisbane 9, 18, 19, 32
Broken Hill 16
bushfires 9, 38, 39–40

C

Canberra 9, 26
capitalism 9
cattle 9, 29, 30–31, 38
Central Plains 10, 11
cities 9, 18, 32–33, 36, 42
climate 12–13, 43
coal 9, 16, 17, 33
convicts 8, 27
Coober Pedy 16, 23
copper ore 16
corroboree 20, 21
crocodiles 40
cyclones 9, 12

D

Darling, River 9, 11
Darling Downs 30–31
Darwin 12, 13, 19
desertification 9, 39–40
deserts 10, 13, 39, 40
didgeridoo 20
doctors 23, 25, 36
droughts 9, 14
dust storms 13–14

E

Eastern Highlands 10, 11, 15, 17
education 22–23, 25
Elizabeth II, Queen 26, 42
Eyre, Lake 14

F

farming 9, 22, 28–31, 42–43
festivals 24
fishing 31
flag 27
food 31
forestry products 17

G

gold 9, 16, 33
Goldsworthy, Mount 16
government 26–27, 42
Great Artesian Basin 11, 17
Great Barrier Reef 11, 35, 38
Great Dividing Range 10, 28
groundwater 17

H

health 23
Hobart 19, 25, 33
hospitals 25
Hotham, Mount 11

I

immigrants 8–9, 18–21
industry 9, 32–33, 43
iron ore 9, 16
irrigation 11, 39

K

Kalgoorlie 16
kangaroos 39
koalas 40
Koolan Island 16
Kosciusko, Mount 9

L

lakes 14

landscape 10–11

M

mangroves 40
Melbourne 9, 18, 19, 32
mining 9, 16–17, 43
mountains 9, 15
Murray-Darling river system 11

N

New South Wales 18, 28, 29, 30
Northern Territory 10, 13, 27, 38
Nullabor Plain 10, 36

O

Oodnadatta 13
opals 16, 17
outback 10, 16, 25, 31, 42

P

pavlova 31
Perth 9, 13, 18, 19, 42
petroleum 16
Pinnacles Desert 40
plants 38, 40
police 27
population 9, 18–21, 42, 43
ports 36–37

Q

Qantas 36
Queensland 18, 30, 31, 33, 34, 38

R

railroads 36, 37
rainfall 13–15
religion 9, 22
rivers 14, 37
road trains 37
roads 36, 37
Roxby Downs 16

Royal Flying Doctor Service 23, 36

S

salinization 9, 39
School of the Air 23, 25, 43
Shark Bay 35
sheep 9, 28, 29, 30–31, 38
skin cancer 14–15
Snowy Mountains 15, 17
South Australia 28, 30
sports 23–25
sugarcane 29, 30
Surfers Paradise 34
Sydney 9, 13, 18, 19, 25, 32–33, 37, 39
Sydney Harbor 8, 24, 35
Sydney Opera House 8, 35

T

Tasman Sea 15
Tasmania 11, 15, 22, 38
tourism 35
trade 32–34
transportation 9, 36–37

U

Uluru (Ayers Rock) 8, 10, 35, 38, 43

V

Victoria 17, 18, 28, 29
vineyards 9, 28

W

water 11, 17, 39
weather 12–15, 43
Western Australia 16, 18, 30, 35, 40
Western Plateau 10
wheat 9, 28–30, 33
wool 9, 28, 29, 33

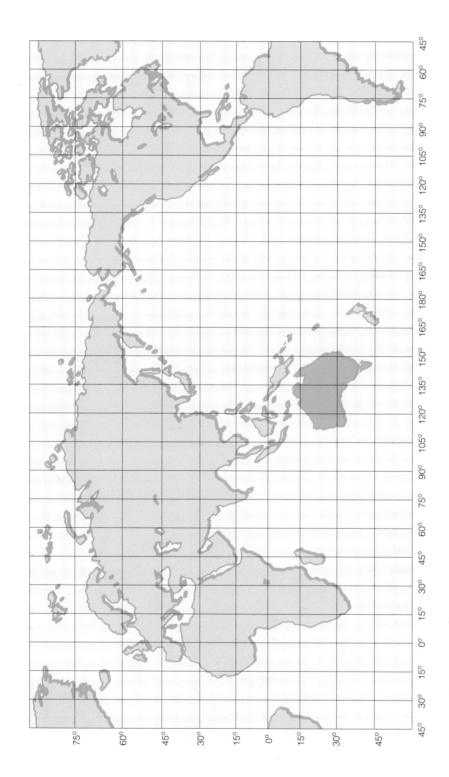

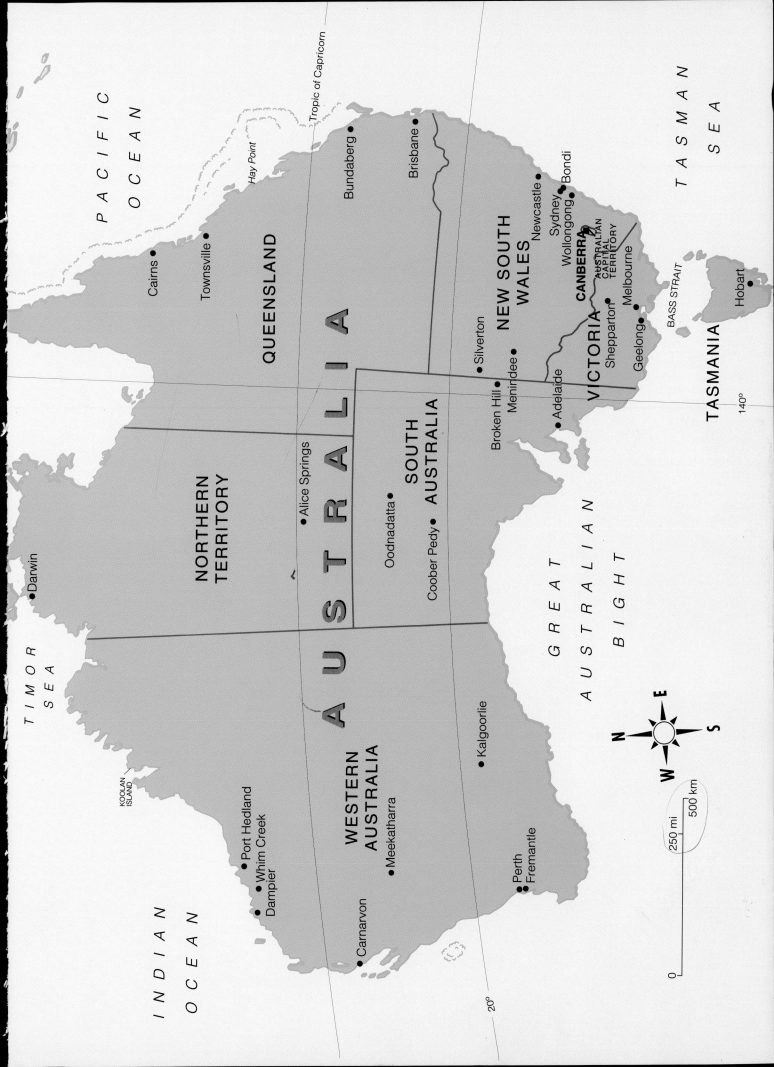